*All the Light We Cannot See*, the second novel from Anthony Doerr, takes place during World War II. It tells the story of a young, blind girl living in Paris with her father. The pair must escape as the War nears Paris, but not without taking the precious, and highly sought after, Sea of Flames. Marie-Laure and her father travel to Saint-Malo to live with Uncle Etienne and Madame Manec.

On the other side of the story, Werner Pfennig is a young boy growing up in Germany. He takes a special interest in electronics and radios. He becomes so skilled that he gains the attention of the Nazis and enters their training program. He eventually arrives in Saint-Malo and must make a decision that will change the life of Marie-Laure.

*All the Light We Cannot See* gained worldwide attention when it won the Pulitzer Prize for Fiction in 2015 and was a finalist for the National Book Award in 2014.

# Conversation Starters

for

## Anthony Doerr's

# All the Light We Cannot See

## By Read2Lead

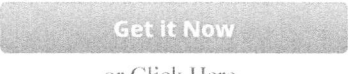

**Tips for Using Read2Lead Conversation Starters:**

EVERY GOOD BOOK CONTAINS A WORLD FAR DEEPER THAN the surface of its pages. The characters and their world come alive through the words on the pages, yet the characters and its world still live on. Questions herein are designed to bring us beneath the surface of the page and invite us into the world that lives on. These questions can be used to:

- Foster a deeper understanding of the book
- Promote an atmosphere of discussion for groups
- Assist in the study of the book, either individually or corporately
- Explore unseen realms of the book as never seen before

**About Us:**

THROUGH YEARS OF EXPERIENCE AND FIELD EXPERTISE, from newspaper featured book clubs to local library chapters, *Read2Lead* can bring your book discussion to life. Host your book party as we discuss some of today's most widely read books.

## Table of Contents

# Introducing *All the Light We Cannot See*

*ALL THE LIGHT WE CANNOT SEE* TAKES PLACE DURING WORLD WAR II. THE stories of two young people are told, giving two incredibly different perspectives during the War: Marie-Laure Leblanc, a young child who must escape Paris, France, and Werner Pfennig, a child in Germany who grows up to join the Nazis. The story takes place over the span of ten years from 1934 to 1944.

In 1934, Marie-Laure Leblanc is living in Paris, France, with her father. Her father works as a locksmith. As the war moves closer to Paris, Daniel is asked to make three copies of a precious stone that is never shown to the public called the Sea of Flames. The real stone and its copies are then given to four couriers. The four people do not know whether they have the real stone or not. Daniel ends up receiving one of the stones.

Marie-Laure lost her sight as a young child. To help her, Daniel created a model of their house and their neighborhood. Marie-Laure is eventually able to navigate the area they live in confidently. However, that all changes when Daniel and Marie-Laure must leave Paris and escape to Saint-Malo. Marie-Laure feels afraid at the thought of leaving her home and the safety of knowing the area where she lives.

Marie-Laure and Daniel arrive in Saint-Malo where they live with her uncle Etienne and Madame Manec. Daniel promises that he will never leave Marie-Laure, and he begins to build her a model of the house in Saint-Malo.

In Germany in 1934, Werner Pfennig and his sister Jutta are orphans living in an orphanage in Zollverein. Werner takes great interest in a radio program hosted by a man in France, and he begins to teach himself about electronics. He eventually learns how to build his own radios.

When word travels around about Werner's skill in electronics and radios, he is put into a Nazi training program at the National Political Institutes of Education. He hates the training he is receiving and wishes he could be back with his sister Jutta. However, he is eventually put in charge of finding people who are sending illegal radio signals.

In 1944, Werner's unit arrives in Saint-Malo. Their mission is to find the person sending illegal intelligence broadcasts and destroy them. Von Rumpel is also on the island with a mission to find the Sea of Flames. His motivation to find the stone is that he believes it will cure the cancer he is dying from. Daniel and Etienne are both captured from the house leaving Marie-Laure alone.

Werner discovers the source of the radio broadcasts and learns that they are the same broadcasts he listened to as a child that inspired his interest in electronics. The man he had been inspired by since childhood was Marie-Laure's Uncle Etienne. Werner decides to save Marie-Laure from von Rumpel and gets her to safety. However, Werner becomes extremely ill and one night he mistakenly steps on a landmine, which kills him instantly.

Thirty years after Werner's death, Jutta meets with Marie-Laure. Marie-Laure learns that Werner left the Sea of Flames in the grotto in Saint-Malo. The story ends with Marie-Laure as an elderly woman living in Paris.

# Introducing the Author

ANTHONY DOERR WAS BORN IN CLEVELAND, OHIO, IN 1973. HE SPENT much of his childhood in Novelty, Ohio. Novelty, also known as Russel Township, is a small town of just over 5,000 people in northeastern Ohio. Doerr attended the prestigious secondary school known as University School in nearby Cuyahoga County, Ohio. He graduated from University School in 1991.

After leaving his secondary school, Doerr moved to Brunswick, Maine, where he attended Bowdoin College. At Bowdoin College, Doerr was a history major. He graduated from Bowdoin College in 1995 with a bachelor of arts. He later went on to study at Bowling Green State Universitywhere he obtained a master of fine arts.

Before becoming a novelist, Doerr wrote mainly short stories. He published his first collection of short stories in 2002. This collection was called *The Shell Collector*. Many of the stories found in *The Shell Collector*are set in New Zealand and Africa. Doerr has lived and worked in both locations.

In 2010, Doerr released another collection of short stories called *Memory Wall*. The stories found in *Memory Wall* take place across the world from Wyoming to South Africa to Lithuania. The collection won many awards including the Notable Book of 2010 Award from *The New York Times* and the National Magazine Award for the title novella in the collection.

In 2004, Doerr's first novel, *About Grace*, was published. *About Grace* tells the story of David Winkler, a hydrologist. David often has dreams that come true later in his life. *About*

*Grace* was chosen as one of The Book-of-the-Month Club's top five books of 2004. It was also a Book of the Year selection for *The Washington Post*.

In 2014, Doerr gained a large amount of attention for his popular book release, *All the Light We Cannot See*. The story went on to win the Pulitzer Prize for Fiction in 2015. It was also a National Book Award finalist and was named as a notable book of 2014 by *The New York Times*.

# *Discussion Questions*

. . . . . . . . . . . . . . . . . . . . . . . . . . .

### question 1

*All the Light You Cannot See* often switches perspectives from Marie Laure's point of view to Werner's point of view. Did this make it difficult for you to follow along while reading? Do you think the story should have been told in a different way? Why or why not?

. . . . . . . . . . . . . . . . . . . . . . . . . . .

. . . . . . . . . . . . . . . . . . . . . . . . . . . . .

## question 2

*All the Light You Cannot See* changes between Marie-Laure's point of view and Werner's point of view. Did you enjoy the perspective of either one more than the other? If so, which one did you prefer and why?

. . . . . . . . . . . . . . . . . . . . . . . . . . . .

. . . . . . . . . . . . . . . . . . . . . . . . . . . . . . .

**question 3**

Werner eventually goes on to become part of the Nazis in Germany. Why do you think he did this? Do you think he had a choice? Why or why not?

. . . . . . . . . . . . . . . . . . . . . . . . . . . . . . .

. . . . . . . . . . . . . . . . . . . . . . . . . . . . . . . .

## question 4

*All the Light You Cannot See* takes place in Germany and France during World War II. What did you learn about World War II from this story? Do you think it is a factual representation of the actual events that took place during this time?

. . . . . . . . . . . . . . . . . . . . . . . . . . . . . . . .

. . . . . . . . . . . . . . . . . . . . . . . . . . . . .

## question 5

When the Nazis arrive on Saint-Malo, Marie-Laure is living there with her
father and uncle. Werner makes the decision to save Marie-Laure. Why do
you think he chose to do this? Do you think that there were other members of
the Nazis who would have done the same? Why or why not?

. . . . . . . . . . . . . . . . . . . . . . . . . . . . .

. . . . . . . . . . . . . . . . . . . . . . . . . . . . .

## question 6

Anthony Doerr often gives glimpses into the future of the characters' lives throughout *All the Light We Cannot See*. Did you like that Doerr wrote the book in this way? Would you have preferred the novel to be written in chronological order? Why or why not?

. . . . . . . . . . . . . . . . . . . . . . . . . . . .

.

### question 7

In the novel, Madame Manec states that "doing nothing is a kind of troublemaking." Do you agree with this statement? Why or why not?

. . . . . . . . . . . . . . . . . . . . . . . . . . . . .

## question 8

In the novel, Madame Manec asks, "Do you want to be alive before you die?"
What do you think she meant by this statement? Explain your answer.
. . . . . . . . . . . . . . . . . . . . . . . . . . .

. . . . . . . . . . . . . . . . . . . . . . . . . . . . . .

## question 9

In the novel, Madame Manec uses an analogy of a boiling frog. Later on,
Etienne asks Marie-Laure who the frog is supposed to represent. What do you
think is the meaning behind the boiling frog analogy? Who was the frog in
your opinion?

. . . . . . . . . . . . . . . . . . . . . . . . . . . . . .

. . . . . . . . . . . . . . . . . . . . . . . . . . . . . . . .

## question 10

Etienne lived his life as a recluse, far away from anything he perceived as a danger. He believed he was safe, far away from the world. However, the Nazis came to the island he lived on, Saint-Malo, anyway. How do you think this event relates to Madame Manec saying, "Do you want to be alive before you die?" Do you agree with Etienne's choice to live far away from other people? Why or why not?

. . . . . . . . . . . . . . . . . . . . . . . . . . . . . . .

## question 11

Frederick was demanded by family to join the Nazi school. Why do you think his family pushed him to attend the school?

. . . . . . . . . . . . . . . . . . . . . . . . . . . . . . . . .

## question 12

The Sea of Flames is a precious gem that must be guarded throughout the novel. Marie-Laure's family is the protector of the Sea of Flames. Where does the Sea of Flames end up at the novel's conclusion? Do you think Werner knew the location of the Sea of Flames? If so, why do you think he kept it a secret?

. . . . . . . . . . . . . . . . . . . . . . . . . . . . . . . . .

. . . . . . . . . . . . . . . . . . . . . . . . . . . . . . .

## question 13

The title is *All the Light We Cannot See*. The motifs "light" and "see" show
up multiple places in the novel. Marie-Laure is completely unable to see.
What do you think the meaning of the book title is? What is the "light we
cannot see" referring to?

. . . . . . . . . . . . . . . . . . . . . . . . . . . . . . .

· · · · · · · · · · · · · · · · · · · · · · · · · · · · · ·

## question 14

The reader never finds out exactly what happened to Marie-Laure's father. There is no record of his death. What do you think happened to him? Why do you think the author chose to end his story in this way? Do you think this was common during World War II for families to never know what happened to certain family members?

· · · · · · · · · · · · · · · · · · · · · · · · · · · · · ·

. . . . . . . . . . . . . . . . . . . . . . . . . . . . . .

### question 15

In the novel, when Marie-Laure meets with Jutta, she never tells Jutta that
Werner saved her life. Why do you think she chose to do this?
. . . . . . . . . . . . . . . . . . . . . . . . . . . . . .

. . . . . . . . . . . . . . . . . . . . . . . . . . . . . . .

## question 16

A few readers felt as though the book was difficult to understand because of
the complex wording and analogies Anthony Doerr uses throughout the story.
Do you agree with this statement? Did you struggle to understand the novel?
Do you think the story would have been as effective if it were writing in
simpler language?

. . . . . . . . . . . . . . . . . . . . . . . . . . . . . .

. . . . . . . . . . . . . . . . . . . . . . . . . . . . . . . .

## question 17

Some readers were upset and disappointed by the death at the end of the novel. How did you feel about the novel's ending? Why do you think the author chose to end it in this way?

. . . . . . . . . . . . . . . . . . . . . . . . . . . . . .

. . . . . . . . . . . . . . . . . . . . . . . . . . . . . .

## question 18

Some readers felt the rape scene in the novel was unnecessary. Others felt that it showed historical accuracy and therefore, was essential to the novel's plot because people should know the truth about war. They felt the reader should also see that war is difficult for the civilians as well as the soldiers. How do you feel about this scene? Do you think it was necessary or unnecessary for the plot? Explain your answer.

. . . . . . . . . . . . . . . . . . . . . . . . . . . . . .

. . . . . . . . . . . . . . . . . . . . . . . . . . . . . . . .

**question 19**

Many readers felt frustrated that Jutta did not form close relationships or a bond with Volkheimer or Marie-Laure. Do you share this feeling? Why or why not?

. . . . . . . . . . . . . . . . . . . . . . . . . . . . . . . .

· · · · · · · · · · · · · · · · · · · · · · · · · · · · · · ·

## question 20

*All the Light We Cannot See* was a *New York Times* bestseller and won The Pulitzer Prize for Fiction. Do you think the story deserved this level of recognition? Why or why not?

· · · · · · · · · · · · · · · · · · · · · · · · · · · · · · ·

. . . . . . . . . . . . . . . . . . . . . . . . . . . . . .

## question 21

Some readers felt the book was difficult to begin reading, so they stopped reading it for a while. Then, they picked it up at a later date and found it interesting. When you began reading the story, did you want to give up and read something else? Why or why not?

. . . . . . . . . . . . . . . . . . . . . . . . . . . . . .

. . . . . . . . . . . . . . . . . . . . . . . . . . . . . .

**question 22**

A few readers felt as though the story took too long to become interesting. They also felt as if they were always waiting for something important to happen, but it took too long to get to the important part of the story. Do you agree with this statement? Why or why not?

. . . . . . . . . . . . . . . . . . . . . . . . . . . . . .

. . . . . . . . . . . . . . . . . . . . . . . . . . . . . .

## question 23

A few readers felt as though it was confusing for Anthony Doerr to write the story by flipping back and forth between time periods. Do you agree with that statement? Did you find the story confusing? Why or why not?

. . . . . . . . . . . . . . . . . . . . . . . . . . . .

. . . . . . . . . . . . . . . . . . . . . . . . . . . .

## question 24

Many readers felt as though this story would be widely loved by a large audience because of the story line. Do you agree with this statement? Why or why not?

. . . . . . . . . . . . . . . . . . . . . . . . . . . .

. . . . . . . . . . . . . . . . . . . . . . . . . . . . . . .

## question 25

One reader described this story as a "unique" and "beautiful" story of World War II. With all of the books available about World War II, the Nazis, and Jewish people in concentration camps, do you agree that *All the Light We Cannot See* is unique? Why or why not? What makes it stand out from other World War II stories you have read?

. . . . . . . . . . . . . . . . . . . . . . . . . . . . . .

· · · · · · · · · · · · · · · · · · · · · · · · · · · · ·

## question 26

Anthony Doerr wrote his second novel, *All the Light We Cannot See,* over the course of ten years. Do you feel as though that is an appropriate length of time to write a novel? Do you think the author should have given up and started another story? Why or why not?

· · · · · · · · · · · · · · · · · · · · · · · · · · · · ·

. . . . . . . . . . . . . . . . . . . . . . . . . . . . . . .

## question 27

Anthony Doerr previously wrote short stories. He released two collections of short stories before becoming a novelist. How do you think his experience with writing short stories helped him when writing his first novel?

. . . . . . . . . . . . . . . . . . . . . . . . . . . . . . .

## question 28

Anthony Doerr grew up in a small town in Ohio. He attended a prestigious secondary school in a town nearby. Do you think his childhood experiences helped him in his career as an author? Why or why not?

## question 29

Anthony Doerr studied history at Bowdoin College and later earned a bachelor of arts and a master of fine arts. Do you think Doerr's knowledge of history helped him in his career as a writer? Why or why not? Do you think attending college helped him in his career as a writer? Why or why not?

. . . . . . . . . . . . . . . . . . . . . . . . . . . . . . . .

**question 30**

Anthony Doerr often writes stories that take place outside of the United
States, where he grew up. Do you think any events from his life may have
inspired him to choose stories set in other countries? Why or why not? What
events do you think may have inspired him?

. . . . . . . . . . . . . . . . . . . . . . . . . . . . . . .

. . . . . . . . . . . . . . . . . . . . . . . . . . . . . .

## question 31

In the novel, Madame Manec states that "doing nothing is a kind of troublemaking." What do you think would have happened in the story if more people had risen up and done something? Do you think it could have changed the course of history? Why or why not?

. . . . . . . . . . . . . . . . . . . . . . . . . . . . . .

· · · · · · · · · · · · · · · · · · · · · · · · · · · · · ·

### question 32

In the novel, Marie-Laure never tells Jutta that Werner saved her life. Would you have done the same if you were Marie-Laure? Why or why not? If you were Jutta, would you want to know that your brother saved the life of Marie-Laure?

· · · · · · · · · · · · · · · · · · · · · · · · · · · · · ·

## question 33

Werner did not have the stone with him when he walked into the field of land mines. If Werner did have the stone with him, do you think things would have concluded differently? Do you think he would have been saved? Why or why not?

. . . . . . . . . . . . . . . . . . . . . . . . . . . .

### question 34

If Werner had survived in this novel, do you think he would have returned to retrieve the Sea of Flames? Why or why not?

. . . . . . . . . . . . . . . . . . . . . . . . . . . .

. . . . . . . . . . . . . . . . . . . . . . . . . . . . . . .

## question 35

Daniel and Marie-Laure leave Paris in hopes to escape the war. Most of the journey is dangerous. What do you think would have happened to the two of them had they not escaped Paris? Would you have made the journey to Saint-Malo if you were in the same situation? Why or why not?

. . . . . . . . . . . . . . . . . . . . . . . . . . . . . .

. . . . . . . . . . . . . . . . . . . . . . . . . . . . . . .

### question 36

Werner becomes exceptionally skilled in electronics. This leads to his recruitment by the Nazis. Do you think Werner's story would have a different outcome if his skill had not been discovered or if he had not become skilled at all? Why or why not? If so, in what ways would his life be different?

. . . . . . . . . . . . . . . . . . . . . . . . . . . . . . .

## question 37

In the novel, Werner saves Marie-Laure from von Rumpel. What do you think Marie-Laure's fate would have been had Werner not saved her?

· · · · · · · · · · · · · · · · · · · · · · · · · · ·

· · · · · · · · · · · · · · · · · · · · · · · · · · · · · ·

## question 38

*All the Light We Cannot See* changes perspectives between Marie-Laure and Werner. How do you think the story would be different if only one side of the story was told? Do you think the story would be as effective? Why or why not?

· · · · · · · · · · · · · · · · · · · · · · · · · · · · · ·

# *Quiz Questions*

. . . . . . . . . . . . . . . . . . . . . . . . . . . . . . . .

### question 39

The two main characters of *All the Light We Cannot See* are _____
and _____.

. . . . . . . . . . . . . . . . . . . . . . . . . . . . . . . .

. . . . . . . . . . . . . . . . . . . . . . . . . . . .

**question 40**

Marie-Laure relocates to Saint-Malo with her _____ and lives
with her _____.

. . . . . . . . . . . . . . . . . . . . . . . . . . .

. . . . . . . . . . . . . . . . . . . . . . . . . . .

## question 41

Werner became skilled in electronics and went on to become a member of the
_____.

. . . . . . . . . . . . . . . . . . . . . . . . . .

. . . . . . . . . . . . . . . . . . . . . . . . . . . . . . . .

### question 42

**True or False:** Werner risked his life to save Marie-Laure's life.
. . . . . . . . . . . . . . . . . . . . . . . . . . . . . . . .

## question 43

**True or False:** Marie-Laure lives in France.

. . . . . . . . . . . . . . . . . . . . . . . . . . . . . . .

### question 44

**True or False:** Werner lives in Belgium.

. . . . . . . . . . . . . . . . . . . . . . . . . . . . . .

## question 45

**True or False:** *All the Light We Cannot See* takes place during World War I.

## question 46

Anthony Doerr was born and raised in a small town. This town was located in
_____.

## question 47

Anthony Doerr received a bachelor of arts and a masters of fine arts. Doerr
studied _____ at Bowdoin College.

. . . . . . . . . . . . . . . . . . . . . . . . . . .

**question 48**

Anthony Doerr focused on writing short stories before becoming a novelist.
Doerr's first collection of short stories was called
_____.

. . . . . . . . . . . . . . . . . . . . . . . . . . .

. . . . . . . . . . . . . . . . . . . . . . . . . . . . . . .

## question 49

**True or False:** Anthony Doerr wrote his first novel in 2004. This novel was called *All the Light We Cannot See*.

. . . . . . . . . . . . . . . . . . . . . . . . . . . . . .

. . . . . . . . . . . . . . . . . . . . . . . . . . . . . .

### question 50

**True or False:** *All the Light We Cannot See* gained a large amount of attention worldwide. It was also the winner of the Pulitzer Prize for Fiction in 2015.

. . . . . . . . . . . . . . . . . . . . . . . . . . . . . .

# *Quiz Answers*

1.  Werner and Marie-Laure

2.  father; uncle

3.  Nazis

4.  True

5.  True

6.  False; Werner is from Germany

7.  False; It takes place during World War II.

8.  Ohio

9.  history

10. The Shell Collector

11. False; his first novel was *About Grace*

12. True

# THE END

# Want to promote your book group? Register here.

Printed in Great Britain
by Amazon

74415934R00041